Shortcuts to

finding your
get up and go

Thorsons
An Imprint of HarperCollins*Publishers*
77–85 Fulham Palace Road,
Hammersmith, London W6 8JB

The Thorsons website address is: www.thorsons.com

and *Thorsons*
are trademarks of
HarperCollins*Publishers* Ltd

First published by Thorsons 2002

1 3 5 7 9 10 8 6 4 2

© Gael Lindenfield 2002

Gael Lindenfield asserts the moral right to be
identified as the author of this work

A catalogue record of this book is
available from the British Library

ISBN 0 00 710052 3

Printed and bound in Great Britain by
Clays Ltd, St. Ives plc

Shortcuts to
finding your get up and go

Gael Lindenfield

Thorsons

To John Wright

With love and thanks for the wonderful
hospitality of your house which stands as a
testament to your ability to get going
in spite of it all!

Acknowledgements for the
Shortcuts Series

First, thanks again to all the people who have so openly shared their struggles with me. I hope that you will be pleased that the wisdom I gained from your difficult experiences has been constructively channelled into these Shortcut strategies.

Secondly, many special thanks to Jo Kyle who has done such a magnificent job with the editing of these books. Working with Jo in cyberspace has opened my eyes up to the amazing potential of electronic relationships. I have learned to trust and respect the judgement of someone simply through the exchange of written words. (A good lesson for a writer!)

Thirdly, the Thorsons team has been as patient, supportive and willing to experiment as ever. A big thank you to each and every one of you.

Fourthly, *muchas gracias a mis amigos en La Puebla de Los Infantes* who fed and entertained me so often while I was in Spain writing much of this series. You were an inspiration as well as a support.

Finally, once again my husband Stuart's contribution must be acknowledged. The title of this series was his idea. As ever, I am also grateful to him for giving over so much of his precious free time to edit my dyslexic manuscripts before they leave the privacy of our home.

Other titles in the series:

Contents

Introduction to the
Shortcuts Series

At this moment in your life, reading a book is probably one of the last things you feel like doing. If so, you are exactly the kind of reader I had in mind when I designed this Shortcuts series!

I have struggled with enough personal problems myself to know that when you are in the throes of them, the thought of wading through any book is daunting. You just haven't got the concentration or the motivation. When I am in this situation, all I long for is for someone to tell me what to do – or, even better, relieve me of my hurt or worry by taking it away from me!

So I would like you to think of these Shortcuts guides not so much as books but as supportive *tools*. I do not intend them to be like an absorbing 'read' to take to the sofa or bath and get 'lost' in. On the contrary, they are designed as 'ready-made' strategies to help kick you into action – and to keep you moving over a period of one to two months – at least! (Isn't 'the getting going' always the hardest part of solving any problem? This is when I have found that even the most competent and self-reliant people can benefit from support.)

But it is also important that when we do get started, we begin in a *constructive* way. A common mistake is to *do* the first thing that comes into our mind. This can make us feel better because we *feel* more in control. But this 'hit and miss' approach often gets us going on a very much longer and rockier road than we need have taken. In contrast, these Shortcut strategies will guide you along a route that has been meticulously planned. They are derived from years of experimentation and studying other people's tried and tested paths.

The first characteristic of each book that you may notice (and perhaps find initially frustrating) is that they all start with some preparation work. This is because, in my experience, diving headlong into the heart of the problem often proves to be the shortcut to failure!

After you have prepared yourself, the strategy moves along in a series of small steps. Although sometimes these steps will overlap, most of the time you should find that one naturally follows on from the other. At the end of each, you will find a list of tips called 'Action time!'. Some of the suggestions and exercises in this section may work better for you than others. But I am confident that in the process of trying them, you are much more likely to find out what *will* help than if you did nothing at all! So I hope you will find them of use one way or another.

Throughout the book you will also find some quotes and key 'messages' (highlighted in bold type). I hope you will find these useful should you just want to dip into the book and gain some quick support and guidance at times when the going feels tough.

Finally, I would like you to always bear in mind that in the personal development field there are no prizes for being first to the winning post. But there are, however, plenty of rewards to be had from the *effective* learning of problem-solving skills. So if you proceed through these Shortcuts books at a pace which feels *comfortably challenging*, you will have

learned an invaluable skill that could save you time
and energy for the rest of your life.

Enjoy the journey! (Yes, problem solving *can* be
highly pleasurable!)

Introduction

'Just do it!'

Do you feel like wiping that goading nineties slogan off the face of the planet right now?! Aren't you sick to death of having it thrown in your face and ears by the overly bright and breezy go-getters of this world. *'If only it were that easy!'* is the understandable enraged response I hear from so many people who are stuck unhappily in their own rut.

Or perhaps you are too full of apathy already to be irritated or goaded by such simplistic moralizing.

Either reaction would indicate that you are on the right track. You need this book!

You are probably too angry or too fed up with yourself to be able to get going without some help to re-light your motivational fire. But that 'help' needs to be of a certain kind. Compassionate doses of sympathy, encouraging reminders of your goals and resolutions or well-meaning threats have probably already made you feel worse *not* better. What you need is a down-to-earth action strategy which will draw on your own unique set of strengths and aspirations.

How can I say this with such confidence? Firstly, I have found my way out of plenty of ruts myself, but the last major one I was in was over 30 years ago. Secondly, since that time I have helped many thousands of others find their own path out of their ruts. Thirdly, I am convinced that the reason why I am so successful in this aspect of my work is that I find it *personally* fulfilling. It uses and develops my own personal strengths and I find the challenge endlessly stimulating. (Each of us is so unique in regard to what makes us tick into action – how could I ever get bored?)

So, not surprisingly, this strategy is essentially an individualized adventure in self-exploration. The wisdom, however, that has been used to design its outline plan and action exercises is drawn from the real-life experiences of many others.

A deep understanding of yourself and your wants and needs is one of the most important keys to self-motivation – and that is the *only* kind of motivation that will keep you well clear of ruts in the future. You probably already know how easy it is to be 'shocked' or 'irresistibly enticed' out of most ruts for a *short* while. But you wouldn't be reading this book if you didn't also know how it is even easier to slide back in there if you over-depend on external factors provided by others to keep you going.

I expect readers will have picked up this book for many different reasons. You could be, for example:

- stuck in a job that is boring you silly or holding you back
- unable to persist with a diet or exercise regime which you know you need
- endlessly putting off starting the hobby or sport that you have always wanted to do

- sick of talking about a life-dream that you never do anything about realizing
- feeling trapped in a relationship that is growing staler and staler by the hour
- getting unbearably envious of the success of a friend who appears to have less talent than nature or nurture gave you
- being bypassed for promotion because your boss says you don't have the 'oomph' the business needs
- suffering from the shock of a trauma that has acted as a 'wake-up' call, but you haven't a clue how to start changing yourself or your life

So your problem situations may indeed be very different, but undoubtedly the self-sabotaging feelings arising from not getting going on tackling them is much the same. And that's what this book will help you tackle. It guides you along a journey that will keep you in action while also building up your internal motivational muscles. Some of you may of course need a stronger and longer 'workout' than others to get going and keep going consistently. There will be those of you who have been struggling with this problem for most of your life, while others could well be experiencing your first ever serious motivational 'dip'.

Also, much will depend on the causes behind your difficulties. These can be very deeply embedded in your personality. (For example, chronic low self-esteem or a fear of change as a result of a difficult childhood; a predisposition towards becoming anxious or frequent depression, or a phlegmatic temperament inherited through your genes.) Alternatively, the chief cause of your problem could be a current overload of the kind of stress which would depress the motivation of almost anyone. (For example, being compelled to do an unrewarding job for an overly long period; being the subject of a series of major losses or rejections, or living in the company of negative people who are themselves stuck in major ruts and feel powerless to change their lives.)

But I am guessing that what everyone who has begun to read this book shares is the need for a powerful 'kick-start' – the kind which will keep you going long enough to enjoy being in action so much that you will be determined to do whatever it takes to keep you from going back into that rut. This is what this Shortcut strategy offers.

What is the
Shortcut Strategy?

As you will see, our Shortcut strategy for finding your get up and go is divided into four stages:

STAGE 1: **Getting Prepared**
STAGE 2: **Giving Yourself a Refreshing Recharge**
STAGE 3: **Getting Your Destination More Clearly in Sight**
STAGE 4: **Making it Easy to Keep Yourself Going**

As I mentioned in the general introduction to this series, within each of these stages there are a number of different steps to work through. You will notice I have not included specific time guidelines for completing each step. This is because each of you will be working at your own individual pace. Some of you may even want to skip an occasional step or exercise if it is not relevant to you or your lifestyle. As I said earlier, the strategy will take most people around two months to complete if you set aside approximately one to two hours per week to work through the suggestions and exercises. But if you find you need longer, I trust that you will not abandon the strategy just because Mr and Ms Average have managed to work faster than you! (Your life after all could be much more fascinatingly complex than theirs!)

By the end of the strategy I believe that everyone should find it easier than they have done in the past to keep themselves going. So in working through this book you are in effect giving yourself two treatments for the price of one – a quick-fix pep pill, and essential maintenance medication as well. I hope you enjoy using the bargain!

Stage One

getting prepared

You cannot hope to get going without committing a fair degree of mental energy and time to boosting your motivation. So this stage is about preparing your mind and your diary for the work of this Shortcut strategy. You need to make quality space in both!

The first step will help you unload some of the debilitating worry and negativity that is probably clogging up your mind, and replace this with positive encouraging thoughts. The second will help you unload some of the tasks that you feel you *should* do over the next couple of months so that you have some space for doing what you *want* to do.

We cannot change anything unless
we accept it. Condemnation does
not liberate, it oppresses.

CARL JUNG

STEP 1

Stop trying so hard!

It may seem strange to start by shifting your focus away from what it is you are attempting to do. But I hope that you will trust that this is what your first step must be.

In a recent clearout of our family papers, my brother came across my old school reports. Almost every entry by the PE teachers included the words 'She should try harder.' No wonder I never became a sports champion and no wonder I have such problems motivating myself to do any physical exercise which in any way resembles the games lessons I endured at school! Of course I was trying as hard as I possibly could. (Couldn't they see the good-conduct badges that I ensured I earned each year?!)

And I expect you have been trying your best too. I doubt very much that you are the lazy type either. (I am taking an informed guess that you wouldn't be reading this if you hadn't already used every trick in your own book to get yourself moving.)

Bullying yourself into action won't work – indeed it will make you even more stuck. Maybe you know exactly why you have got into this position. But then, perhaps you don't and are desperately trying to understand why you can't get going. It doesn't really matter either way. Right now, neither insight nor tracing the 'culprits' will be of any more help than trying harder. You are too stressed to benefit from any understanding about the cause of your problem.

You are also at risk of becoming depressed. Indeed, you could by now have succumbed. Most people who come to me for help with motivation already have done so. So if you are in a depressed state it is likely that you are convinced that you *deserve* to be shamed and punished. In this 'mode' of thinking, your eyes and ears will only see and hear the information that will 'prove' just how incorrigible you are. For example, you might only hear the criticisms of you from the 'games teacher' types and not even notice the deserved praise coming from others. This is because subconsciously you are looking for 'proof' that you are a 'hopeless case' who deserves to be punished by both the outside world – and, indeed, yourself.

Are you currently wasting your precious energy kicking yourself for not trying hard enough and endlessly wondering why you can't just be the go-getting person you want to be?

If so, there is a strong chance that you have also had some negative messages about you and your motivation planted in your brain during its formative young years. At some stage it might indeed be interesting to try and discover what these were exactly. They could be general 'downers' about your potential or they could be specific to the project you are wanting to engage in right now. But, as I mentioned above, that is a task for the future. In order to get yourself going now you don't *need* that kind of information. (After all, I managed to get going without discovering those school reports for 50 years!)

Your number one task for the moment is to take firmer control of your own mind and mood. Whoever, or whatever, set up those deep-seated neurological patterns which have helped to get you stuck in a motivational slump is no longer in charge. You are! The workings of your brain are now your responsibility. You have the power to re-programme yourself into a more positive encouraging mode. That's what this first crucial step is about.

Take firmer control of your own mind and make it into a friend instead of a foe.

Action time!

- **Ensure that any sabotaging subconscious messages about yourself and your motivation are stifled by constantly bombarding your conscious mind with words of encouragement.** Write down some statements along the lines of the following:

  'Well done for trying'
  'You deserve a break'
  'You have earned the right to rest'
  'You are worthy of respect – whatever!'
  'You don't need to understand why right now'
  'It's ok to do something you find easy and enjoyable first'
  'It's ok to read and need this book – whatever anyone else might think!'

  Put these somewhere where you will 'bump' into them and read them on a regular basis. (For example, the back of the loo door, the kitchen cupboard, the car dashboard or your computer screensaver, to name but a few possible places.)

- **Tell the 'games teacher' types in your life today that you don't need their 'kicks' into action.** Speak firmly and politely to them, but make it very clear that it is encouragement and not bullying that you need. Let them know that you are in the process of getting to grips with your motivation but will do so in your *own* way and at your *own* speed. (And no, they don't need to know you are reading this book. I don't need their put-downs either!)

- **Confide in someone who you know can cheer you on as you work through this strategy.** They need, of course, to be motivated people themselves. If your problem has been long-term, your best support might come from someone who doesn't know the 'old you' too well. (They won't be prejudiced and expect you to fail yet again!) Alternatively, you may be able to find someone who would also like to become more motivated. You could plan to give each other mutual support. This is the basis of the success of many self-help groups and organizations like Weight Watchers.

- **When you find yourself drifting back into trying yet again to get going on whatever it is you are trying to achieve, divert your attention and energy.** Engage yourself in some activity that you thoroughly enjoy doing and which doesn't require a push to get you enthusiastic. If this is something that needs doing, so much the better. (For example, there are even some cleaning and clearing jobs which work as an enjoyable diversion for me. But, as I love dancing, an even more attractive option would be to practise a few tango sequences.)

STEP 2

Test your commitment with time

I am making assumptions again! I am assuming that even though you are not achieving what you want, you may still feel you have too many different demands on your time and energy. You would be in a very unusual position if you didn't feel overloaded. This is such a common 'symptom' amongst those who can't get going. The problem is rarely about not having enough to do. It is more usually about:

- not knowing where or how to start with the many thousands of things you really *want* to do

or,

- having so many uninspiring things you *need* to do that you don't even have time to think of the things you *want* to do.

You may even be well acquainted with both of these positions. (Again, you would not be unusual if you were.) So this step will not be an easy one for you. But, of course, the fact that it isn't easy is all the more reason why it must be done! This book cannot offer you anything unless you can create some space in your life to follow through on the actions suggested for each step.

Did you make enough time for the suggestions and exercises in Step 1?

Probably not – you may have been too eager to get going into the heart of the strategy. An understandable urge but one that must be tamed! That is what this step is for.

Allowing yourself quality time now to work on this strategy will save you years of precious lifetime.

You will never 'find' time for anything. If you want time you must make it.

CHARLES BUXTON

Action time!

- **Review the commitments and free spaces you already have in your diary for the next two months.** Ask yourself if you can make at least one or two hours available for working on this Shortcut strategy each week over the next couple of months. The more time you can spare, the quicker you will get going, of course. But do not aim to finish the strategy in one weekend! It is important that you do some of the tasks over a period of time. For example, many of the exercises are about breaking everyday habits and your new behaviour has to be repeated frequently before it can be 'set' in your personality. So you might think about setting aside a few of your lunchtimes each week or you could devote the best part of one evening on a regular basis.

- **Delegate some of your routine tasks.** For example, find a babysitter to look after your children while you work on this strategy or treat yourself to a gardener or house cleaner for the next few months. (A friend or relative might more than willingly take on a few tasks if they knew it was only for a temporary period and that it would help you to get going.)

- **If you are finding it impossible to set aside this time, ask the person you chose for support for some help.** You obviously need some objectivity! Together you should be able to make some decisions about your priorities. Until you get going in earnest, you can benefit from someone *gently* encouraging you to take more time for yourself. (You will soon see that's what Stage 2 requires in abundance!)

The only way to truly make more time is to say no, schedule less, or cancel appointments. This is called 'self-management' not time-management ... if you don't pilot your own plane someone else will.

CHERYL RICHARDSON

Stage Two

giving yourself a refreshing recharge

Hopefully you have now given up trying to punish yourself into action. You should also have started to give yourself more of that other well-known (but much more efficient) motivator – pleasure. This stage will give you even more of that sweet-tasting medicine, while at the same time renewing your energies. In order to get going you will need to be running well on the four 'cylinders' that fire your motivational 'engine' – i.e. your mind, body, emotions and spirit. Many of the steps are designed to recharge several of these at once. But it is up to you to monitor what is working where. (For example, by asking yourself: *Has my mind been stretched? Is my pulse beating harder? Am I aware of feeling more deeply? Has my spirit been uplifted?*)

Be aware that you need a good balance of all four kinds of energy and that you may find some areas easier and quicker to 'service' than others. (You've already had a clue about my predisposition. Yes, I do find it much less easy to fire up my physical energies than the other three!)

Spoil yourself with sensual pleasure

This is my favourite of many favourite tasks in this stage – not just because of the deep pleasure that it brings, but also for its seemingly magical power to transform me from a vegetable to a human dynamo in such a short time.

But even though I never hesitate to indulge myself with one of these treats when I need to, it still often feels 'wrong'. I can hear myself trying to pretend to the business caller at the other end of the phone that I am not up to my ears in aromatic foam! (Working largely from home, I can indulge in a sensual bath at any time of the day the motivational blues should decide to hit me.) I know I am not alone with my irrational feelings either. The guilty confessions of many other self-employed friends tell all:

'Even though I know I've earned it, every time I book a midday round of golf I have to remind myself that I will work twice as hard that evening to make up for it.'

'When I am curled up in front of my cosy fire with a delicious lunch treat prepared just for me, I can't help feeling wicked. But the wickedness works!'

'I have to confess I found the warm sunshine and blue skies too hard to resist today, so I gave myself the afternoon off.'

There are some even luckier ones who are quite brazen and unashamed about using this kind of indulgence to give themselves a boost.

'This morning I woke with a fit of the blues and I just thought "What the hell!" – and snuggled back under the duvet and blasted my ears out with that amazing new CD I told you about.'

'So here I am sitting at the top of a mountain drinking in the crisp, clean air – it was a spontaneous decision to take a last-minute flight. I knew my brain needed the break.'

And it's no coincidence that each one of these people (the guilty and the guiltless) are amongst the biggest go-getters you are ever likely to meet! Successful self-employment demands the highest quality motivation. We who are 'old-hands' in this game have learned that sensual indulgence is a powerful firing fuel that must be used freely and frequently.

But, of course, we mustn't forget that you can have too much of this good thing and that not *all* sensual pleasures are good for you. (As the coughing cigar smokers and the breathless fancy food fanatics know all too well!)

So this step is about testing out which 'sensible' but still highly pleasurable treats will help to ignite you. (Even if you have found out already, it will do you no harm to enjoy the experiment once again!) You may not have as much freedom as some of my self-employed friends nor the money to indulge in everything you would like to try, but I'm sure there is some way you can give yourself some more of this kind of treat.

Finally, don't forget this kind of medication works just as well with the guilt as without. So don't let that minor emotional irritation become your excuse!

> **Prescribing yourself regular doses of sensual treats is not self-indulgent – it is a sensible habit for all go-getters to develop.**

Learning how to be kind to ourselves, learning how to respect ourselves, is important. The reason that it is important is that when we look into our own hearts, it isn't just ourselves we are discovering. We are also discovering the universe.

ANE PEMA CHÖDRÖN

Action time!

- **Plan a simple sensual 'extra' for yourself** *today*. (For example, a brisk walk or a gentle stroll in a nearby park, a soak in a warm bath or a bracing cool shower followed by a self-massage with a rich body cream, a cool glass of freshly squeezed juice or a steaming mug of dark rich chocolate, half-an-hour listening to beautiful music or glancing through an album or book of stunning pictures.)

- **Plan a treat for yourself to take within the next week or two.** (For example, buy tickets for a concert or exhibition, book yourself into a health farm for half a day, phone a friend who you know would love to 'waste away' an afternoon walking in some beautiful gardens, swimming in a crystal clear pool, sailing through tempestuous challenging waters, invite your nearest and dearest to engage in some other – perhaps unprintable! – sensual pleasure with you!)

- **Write down three ways in which you could increase the pleasure of each of your senses on a regular everyday basis:**

touch – for example, give and receive more hugs, take time to feel and notice contrasting textures of leaves when gardening

sight – for example, change or move the pictures around in your house so you notice them more, select some fresh flowers for your office

sound – listen to music for half-an-hour before getting out of bed, listen to the bird-song or rustle of the leaves in the wind

smell – splash yourself with cologne even when you are not going out anywhere special, buy a jasmine plant

taste – eat more curries, stick to fresh food, go organic

(You can, of course, add the 'sixth sense' **intuition** to this list if you wish. Examples for action on this could be to give yourself more space to get in contact with your gut feelings or to do a daily meditation.)

• **Write down some ideas for one bumper sensual experience for which you could soon start planning (and saving!) for.** (For example, a weekend of Paris nightlife, fishing in a remote

Scottish Loch, snowboarding in the Alps, watching or performing in a live concert, going on a wine-tasting holiday, taking a flight in a hot-air balloon, going white-water rafting, swimming with dolphins.) This treat could double as your reward for getting going at last or it could be an inducement to get you going yet again!

STEP 4

Inspire yourself with new tales of triumph

How motivational have the significant role models in your life been?

Probably not inspiring enough. Go-getters tend to encourage others to become go-getters without apparent effort. And it's not all down to genetics – good example is a proven motivator in itself. The more you have been surrounded by inspirational people, the less likely you are to get stuck in a life rut.

Of course there are exceptions to this rule – and you might be the first to point them out to me! But beware – your vision may be distorted. When I am in this kind of state I know that I have a tendency to think that the whole world is more go-getting than I have ever been.

But even if you have had the most rousing successes staring you in the face throughout your life, perhaps they were just not of the right type to move you in the direction you needed to go in. It could be that the kind of thing you want to do, or achieve, is so different that you have been unable to identify with their example sufficiently. Perhaps you even tried to 'do it their way' and failed, or it made you unhappy. That could be partly why you are in your state. Many people find themselves on the completely wrong track for them for just this reason. (For example, a bored doctor with a top-class surgeon for a father, an unenthusiastic manager in his family's leading-edge business and even apathetic parents following along an established trail of Earth mothers.) If this scenario is familiar to you, remember that no one needs necessarily to be to blamed. (Unless you want to give destiny some 'stick' for dealing you an inappropriate draw!) You just need to get into action and find yourself some other examples which will light your particular fire.

So this step is about bringing yourself into contact with new role models. You may indeed be lucky enough to encounter some of your 'heroes' in real-life, but if this is not possible the paper or screen variety will do just as well for your purpose.

When doing your search, keep in mind the point of the following exercises. They are not designed to send you slavishly following in anyone else's footsteps. You are going to be using their inspiring tales to recharge your motivational batteries in a more general way. And the experiences should be pleasurable. But if hearing a story makes you feel inadequate instead of excited, move on and find another.

Find your own heroes and then you will be inspired and not intimidated by stories of success.

**Lives of great men all remind us
We can make our lives sublime,
And, departing, leave behind us
Footprints on the sands of time.**

HENRY WADSWORTH LONGFELLOW

Action time!

- **Take yourself for an afternoon to your local library or bookstore.** Lose yourself by browsing haphazardly in the autobiography and biography sections. Dip in and out of the books on inspiring people from a wide variety of backgrounds – particularly those different from your own experience. Note down the ones that move or fascinate you most. Then buy or borrow approximately three of these and read them over the next few weeks. On first reading, just enjoy the pleasure you get from 'hearing' the tale told.

- **Treat yourself to a volume of motivational quotes** (see the Recommended Reading list at the end of the book for some suggestions). Read a number each day. Choose a selection of the ones you like best and then try to find out more about the life story of the people who said them. (So ignore those by Mr and Ms Anon!) If you know any TV quiz show addicts, they can be good sources of general knowledge. If they can't help you, try the printed encyclopaedias or do an internet search.

- **If the people you have selected are still alive today, try to make contact with them.** Write to their publishers or producers. Explain what you are trying to do. If these people are truly of the inspirational kind, they will almost certainly have a way of responding encouragingly to such an enquiry – however famous or successful or busy they are! You may even meet someone face-to-face that way.

- **Go backstage after going to concerts, the theatre or other live events and meet the performers you admired.** Have a question such as these ready and waiting: *'Were there any key turning points in your life?'/'What do you do when you have a dip in motivation?'/'Who inspires or inspired you?'*

- **Scan the obituary columns in your newspaper each day.** (No, this is not a depressing thing to do – the life stories are usually very uplifting.)

STEP 5

Excite yourself with enjoyable adventure

Now it is time for some adventure of your own. This step will flex your 'challenge and change' muscles – but with some gentle new experiences rather than a potentially incapacitating high-risk exploit.

Perhaps a few of you have already had one or two of these whilst engaged in Step 3. (A recent swim with dolphins in Mexico was both a sensual and highly adventurous experience for me!) But unless you have already been cured of your inertia, the chances are that you played safe and chose sensual experiences with which you were already familiar.

Is fear of the unknown one of the reasons why you haven't got going?

However much you have learned to hate the rut you are in, you might well be there partly because it feels safe. Even if it doesn't, you could be choosing to burn in a familiar frying pan rather than throw yourself into a more uncertain fire.

You probably don't need me to tell you that if you truly want to get going, you are going to have to look fear straight in the face and deal courageously with it. But maybe you *do* need me to remind you again (remember Step 1?) to go a bit easier on yourself!

Commonly, I find that people in your position have a lifetime habit of pushing themselves too headlong into challenging situations. Or alternatively, they often have just had a recent near-miss experience in the deep end of life which has left them emotionally 'flat'. Whatever the cause, the remedy is the same. And it is not one of the 'bottled' varieties that you may well have already tried. (Pills, alcohol, caffeine, and so on?) You are going to get the adrenalin flowing into your system with graded doses of pleasurable excitement and welcome change. (Don't worry – we will be facing the fear in a head on manner later!)

Motivated people are excited adventurers not fearless buccaneers.

Adventure is the champagne of life.

G. K. CHESTERTON

Action time!

- **Each day, during the next week, make a small change in your routine.** Try, of course, to make sure that the change is more pleasurable rather than less so! (For example, leaving home five to ten minutes earlier and taking a more scenic route, starting your day with an adventure story or an organizational job while listening to music you love, having a better quality lunch in a more lively location, dropping in to see a positive friend or neighbour en route home from work or shopping, taking half an hour to sit down with a great book and refreshing drink before tackling some of your evening chores.) Keep a note of these in your diary or tell a friend to ensure that you do the task and that it is serving its purpose of stimulating excitement. (A trickle of excitement is all that is needed at this stage!)

- **Summon up the courage this week to initiate a conversation with three people whom you haven't talked to before (either at all or very much).** They should of course be people you guess might be interesting company or at least have some knowledge which you don't yet have.

Don't set yourself up for failure with the office or neighbourhood bores or cynics. And remember, excuses such as *'They were all too busy'* or *'I didn't meet anyone new'* are not allowed! Adventurers are proactive – they don't hang around waiting for golden opportunities.

- **Go channel hopping when you are having a TV night at home.** Dip in and out of programmes you wouldn't normally watch – see if you can find some ideas for some more low challenge adventures into activities or places you haven't tried or visited yet. (You could do something similar on the Internet if you prefer.) You may find some ideas so enticing that you want to put them into action.

- **Sign up for a Saturday or evening course in a subject which is an unusual one for you to think about doing.** Most further education departments are very happy for students to test courses out for a couple of weeks and will also be very happy to make some suggestions if you explain your situation to them.

STEP 6

Surround yourself with smiles

After all the work you've done so far in this stage, you certainly ought to be smiling. (You're not? – well, why not backtrack until you are!)

Before moving on to the next step which you may find tougher going, you must ensure that you can maintain your positively recharged state. How often do you hear people say they returned from an uplifting weekend or holiday only to be sucked back down by the long faces of fellow commuters, office colleagues or even their own family?!

Moods are indeed contagious – even the good ones! So this step is about turning this fact to your advantage. You will be actively seeking out 'the smilers' and having less contact with miserable people. If you have been unable to get going for a while it could be that you have been soaking up negativity from other people. You won't even have noticed that you are doing it. Your own sombre face will alone have helped to keep it flowing in your direction!

This does not mean that you have to desert ship and abandon those who may be emotionally sinking or stuck like you were. (You'd be surprised how many people hold themselves back for just this compassionate reason.) Deciding that enough is enough for yourself doesn't immediately transform you into an uncaring or insensitive ogre. But be warned, while you are engaging in this step you may sometimes feel heartless or selfish. And also, you could be perceived by others to be like that. That's tough – but not so tough that it cannot be worked through, especially when you have the support of smiling faces en route.

Once your going is firmly established, you can safely let yourself off this particular hook. You will be more emotionally resilient. And isn't it true that you will also be in a better position to help those who are still stuck? Your inspirational role-modelling alone will have the power to uplift others.

Don't invite negative vibes into your mind – instead, feed yourself with the positive kind.

**Every man is like the company he is
wont to keep.**

EURIPIDES

Action time!

- **Ensure that all the photographs in your house and on your desk are of happy-looking faces.** (These are hard to come by in our family – we all start glaring at the sight of a camera!)

- **Over the next week, cut out pictures from magazines and newspapers and make yourself a large collage of international smiles from people of all ages.** Hang your collage up somewhere where you will see it regularly.

- **Look through some feel-good photography books.** My husband was recently given a brilliant one by a colleague about friendship which was full of smiles that made us smile too.

- **Buy yourself a book of comic poems or quotations or jokes** – read these out loud to friends or relatives who can share a smile with you.

- **Choose a selection of 'happy ending' videos to keep handy when your spirits start to flag.** (Avoid, of course, the overly-sentimental kind that make you squirm not smile.)

STEP 7

Find enticing ways to increase your vigour

Ugh! – not another lecture on the importance of regular exercise and healthy eating!

If that's what you are thinking, I don't blame you. I, for one, have had my own buttons pushed enough on this subject! And it hurts to think that I could have had at least six world cruises with the money I have wasted on gym subscriptions and boring food that passes its sell-by date untouched.

But if I am honest, I will have to admit that all the mass media nagging might have worked. Perhaps it helped to keep me experimenting until at last I found ways to 'shape-up' that I do find enticing. As a result, I guess that in my fifties I must have twice the vigour that I had in my twenties and thirties, so that's not bad going for a reluctant fitness freak, is it?

So I have included this step for those of you who still need some encouragement. (School gym teachers in particular can feel free to skip to the next step!)

There are so many good books, TV programmes, videos and classes around that you certainly don't need specific instructions from me on this theme. So the following few suggestions are just offered as gentle reminders or mind-joggers to stimulate your own ideas.

> **If you feel you are being bullied by yourself or anyone else into any kind of health programme, trust that it is the wrong one for you – but find an attractive alternative quickly.**

That form of exercise is best which not only exercises the body but is also a source of joy to the participant.

GALLEN

Action time!

- **Get dancing!** This must be one of the most enticing ways to exercise. (And no, you don't have to be a good dancer to do this!) Freeing up your body as you move to music – whether you are dancing in public or in the privacy of your home – is a very enjoyable *and* energizing experience. If you choose as difficult and as sensual dances as I have chosen to learn, believe me it can also stretch your mind, spirit and emotions as well! (The Argentine Tango and Spanish Sevillanas are my current challenges, and the Viennese Waltz and Salsa are next on my list.)

- **Make preparations to transform your home into a health farm for a weekend in the very near future.** You could invite a few friends to join you. (Do you have children or a sceptical partner? – well, find minders for both!)

  - A few days before, ruthlessly clear your fridge and cupboards of all unhealthy temptation. (Take them to a neighbour to mind for a few days or you could, of course, give them away forever.)

- Refill the fridge with an excess of *luxury* treats of the kind you know you are allowed. (It's only for one weekend!) Give yourself plenty of scope to 'cheat'. (If healthy, fresh ready-to-eat meals, salads, soups and juices are unavailable in your area – prepare some for yourself a few days before.)
- Fill a giant bowl with exotic fresh fruit salad and another with sticks of fresh vegetables. (These are to dip into *whenever* you like.)
- Buy or borrow a variety of exercise, dance, martial arts, pilates and yoga videos, and plan a programme to watch (and work through!) these.
- Book yourself onto some new outdoor activity that you have been wanting to try – preferably with a lesson so that you will be challenged mentally as well as physically (for example, rowing, sailing or swimming).
- Buy a variety of aromatherapy oils to burn in an oil burner or to add to your bath. Oils such as chamomile, clary sage, frankincense, neroli and lavender are wonderful for relaxation, while basil, eucalyptus, peppermint, pine and rosemary will help to refresh and energize you.

- Arrange for a friend or a mobile therapist to give you a massage.
- Treat yourself to at least one other extravagant 'extra' such as a seaweed scrub to draw out toxins.
- Select some CDs for relaxation sessions.
- Make sure that you have lots of large fluffy towels and comfortable clothing washed and ready to wear.
- Inform the world that you are not at home this weekend!

If all the above sounds too much like hard work, why not treat yourself to the real thing? (At least for a one-day bargain package.)

- **Send your nearest and dearest to Weight Watchers or on a healthy-eating cookery course and let them take over the kitchen as much as possible.** (This is the best personally tried and tested tip of them all!)

Stage Three

getting your destination more clearly in sight

Now that you are feeling more relaxed and nurtured, it is time to get down to taking a serious look at the direction you want to get going in. Maybe it has been hard to see this clearly through the fog of negative feeling that has been created from too much awareness of your weaknesses and fears. So in this stage you will be working on clarifying your strengths, making the vision of your dream more vivid and also mapping out a clearer path to guide your action.

STEP 8

Re-examine your strengths and sharpen your focus on the ones you enjoy

We are much more likely to feel motivated when we are using our best character traits and personal qualities, and we are following what many refer to as our true 'calling' in life.

I hope you agree with this generally accepted truth. Anyway, I am going to presume that you do because I have to! (This is a Shortcut strategy and we haven't the time to refer to the mountain of research papers and biographies it would take to convince a sceptic!)

There are a couple of good reasons why I am suggesting this step now. The first one I am sure you will have guessed. It will boost your self-esteem and you must know how low that is at the moment. You may have even tried the following kinds of exercises before and found they have had very little effect on getting you going. But I believe that if you have faithfully done the work so far in this strategy, you should now be more able to benefit from the confidence they could give you (i.e., you should be more relaxed, less sabotaged and more positive in your outlook).

The second reason is that you may now be more open to discovering that you have been wrong about your true potential and strengths. I have seen that happen so often with my clients that I guess it is also going to be true for many readers of this book. You could have, for example:

- **been trying to get going along a life-path that someone else thought was suited to the potential they saw or wanted to see in you.** (For example, a blinkered teacher who saw the world only in terms of potential danger or a parent who needed you to be famous because they were not)
- **taken a career that was conveniently placed at your doorstep.** And out of habit you have gradually developed some of your 'weaknesses', to a point where they appeared to be your dominant strengths. (For example, a well-paid job

that 'fell into your lap' which you learned to do with ease because it never stretched you)

- **adopted character traits or behaviours in a rebellious mood many years ago to prove a point to someone.** You may have then got so far down a road that you have 'conveniently forgotten' the person you really are. (For example, proving to a sarcastic boss that you *were* management material and forgetting the potential you showed at school for being a radical lone-wolf inventor)
- **started an unsuitable hobby or sport after your best mate talked you into it**

All the above are very easy and human things to do. Many people don't discover they have done them until old age gives them the time to think or the *'What the hell have I got to lose?'* mentality to try being themselves. Hopefully you are not so far down your life-path. (Even if you are, the achievements of the new 'Grey-power' groups should inspire you to continue.)

If you are on the wrong life-path, wouldn't you rather discover and deal with this truth before you reach the land of no-return?

We only do well the things
we like doing.

COLETTE

Action time!

It may help to read through all the tasks in this section before starting to work on it. It could also be helpful to have an overview of the scope of the analysis you are going to do and the amount of paper you may need! Please be aware that you may not be able to enter in answers for every question under the headings whilst for others you may be spoilt for choice.

- **Think of five to six SUCCESSES you have had in your school, university and/or working life to date.** Take a piece of paper (the larger the better!) and divide it into six to seven columns, i.e., one column headed strengths and each of the others headed with one of the successes you have chosen. (See illustration opposite for an example of how to do this.) Enter the answers to the following questions in the appropriate column.

  a) Select up to three of the key **mental strengths** that helped you achieve each success. (For example, memory, analysis, creativity, planning, common sense, and so on.)

Strengths which helped me	Passing my driving test	Last Promotion	Marriage and Home Life
MENTAL	Quick thinking in problem situations	Ability to analyze and think logically	Creative and logical thinking
PHYSICAL	Good eyesight and co-ordination	Stamina	Attractive features and stamina
INTERPERSONAL	Assertively asking for help from the instructor	Good in team	Communication, listening
PERSONAL QUALITIES	Persistence after failing first attempt	Initiative, kind	Nurturing, loving, understanding
KNOWLEDGE	Highway code and knowledge	Degree and training courses	Baby-care, cooking and home finances
LEARNED SKILLS	Relaxation techniques and driving!	Keeping 'difficult' customers happy!	Negotiation and change management

b) Select up to three **physical strengths** or **characteristics** which helped you. (For example, energy, speed, coordination, strength, beauty.)

c) Select up to three **interpersonal skills** which helped you. (For example, listening, leadership, team-working, empathy, compassion, conflict resolution, assertiveness.)

d) Select up to three of the key **character traits** or **personal qualities** which have helped you. (For example, persistence, honesty, trusting, courage, decisiveness.)

e) Select up to three broad categories of **knowledge** or **wisdom**. (For example, mathematical knowledge, life experience of knock-backs, knowledge of literature or music.)

f) Select up to three specific **learned skills** which may have helped you. (For example, ability to ride horses, car maintenance, specific professional or academic training.)

• **Think of five to six other ACHIEVEMENTS you have had.** (For example, in a sport, hobby or community work.) Draw up another page with columns and enter the answers to same questions above in the appropriate column.

- **Think of five to six SATISFYING PERSONAL RELATIONSHIPS you have had or are having.** Draw up another page with columns and enter the answers to the same questions above in the appropriate column.

- **Think of five to six examples of ENJOYABLE and MEMORABLE SOCIAL EVENTS you have experienced in the course of your life.** Draw up another page with columns and enter the answers to the same questions above in the appropriate column.

- **Think of five to six examples of SETBACKS YOU HAVE SUCCESSFULLY OVERCOME in your life.** Draw up another page with columns and enter the answers to the same questions above in the appropriate column.

- **Take some time to study and compare what you have written on each sheet.** You could use different coloured pens to mark the answers to the following kinds of questions you could ask yourself:

- Are there any strong recurring themes?
- Are there any surprising omissions? (For example, maybe you have hardly mentioned your organizational ability or your imagination or compassion.)
- Which of these strengths do you *enjoy* using most?
- Which of these are your key transferable strengths? (For example, you can use them in most situations, work settings, relationships.)
- Which of these enjoyable strengths are most likely to be of help to you in the future you want for yourself?
- Which of these are not being currently used (and could perhaps be resurrected and strengthened)?
- Are there any strengths not listed which you would enjoy using to help develop your potential or achieve what you want to achieve or simply get you going now?

• **Show or talk about your results (as appropriate) to friends or colleagues (peer, senior and junior) and ask for their honest feedback** (i.e. do they agree with your analysis; would they have answered the questions differently from their perception of you and your strengths).

After considering all the assessments, choose a couple of strengths which:

– you particularly enjoy but know could do with being developed
– you believe could help you to keep going on whatever it is that you are wanting to do

• **Write down at least one concrete resolution for each.** For example:

– to develop my creativity, I will set aside one evening a week to writing short stories and book myself onto a painting holiday this summer
– to build on my physical strength, I will treat myself to a series of sessions with a personal trainer

Display this list somewhere highly visible.

STEP 9

Take the paralysis potential out of your fears

Through reacquiring your taste for adventure in Step 5 you have hopefully dealt with at least one of your fears – the one about stepping into the unknown. But there may be several other kinds of fear which are holding you back. Do any of these worries sound familiar to you?

What will ___ think of me if I fail? (Yet again!)

What if I don't like it when I do get going?

What if I lose what I have already got? (And after all, isn't it good-enough?)

What if I get ill and can't stay the course or pay the bills (and someone else has to pick up the pieces)?

What if I make my friends so envious that I cannot handle their backbiting or distancing? (Isn't the price of success inevitably loneliness?)

What if I lose my nerve because I have to do some public speaking or I meet a spider or rat (or encounter any other of my incapacitating phobias)?

What if I change but not for the better? (Don't people often change, especially when they get obsessed with achieving something?)

What if there is another war or an earthquake or an invasion from Mars? (How important am I and my dreams in the grand scheme of things?)

What if it 'is written' that I am going to die tomorrow? (What's the point of it all anyway?!)

And these are just a selection of those that I hear!

Some of the above may sound like pretty 'off the wall' excuses and I admit that it can take the confidentiality of therapy to bring them out into the open. (Particularly the last two which are about facing one's insignificance and mortality.) But it is essential that, at the very least, you do confess your fears to yourself *honestly.* Head-on confrontation has got to be the first step in any strategy designed to manage fears. (And manage them you must, otherwise they will manage you – as indeed they may have been doing for some while!)

But don't forget that the aim of this step is fear control – not eradication. The following suggestions are just a few ways you can do this. There are innumerable others. Some of the books in the Recommended Reading list can also help, as can other kinds of therapy such as hypnosis or, in severe cases, the use of *prescribed* tranquillizers.

Nowadays, any amount of fear is not a good-enough excuse for staying in a rut that doesn't suit you. Don't let yours (or anyone else's) convince you otherwise!

> **Fear is understandable and usually inevitable, but it is never a good-enough excuse for not pursuing your dreams.**

The only things you regret are the things you didn't do.

MICHAEL CURTIZ

Action time!

- **Practise doing the same short relaxation exercise of your choice each day for the next month.** You will find that your brain will start to respond more rapidly the more you practise it. You may need to experiment until you find one that suits you and your lifestyle. Ultimately, you should aim to have mastered at least two techniques which you can use – one for a mini-attack of nerves and the other for a more major panic (see below).

ONE-MINUTE RELAXATION FOR AN ATTACK OF MINI-NERVES

Re-focus your attention immediately on your breathing ensuring that you are breathing deeply and leisurely from your stomach. Slowly repeat a simple calming mantra to yourself several times in time to your breathing. (For example, on your in-breath say 'I am ...' and on your out-breath '... calm.' If you have time, visualize in your mind's eye a calming scene such as the corner of a quiet garden, swans gliding down a river or the sleeping face of a loved one.

Recall the sounds and scents as well (for example, the smell of newly mown grass, the ripple of water or the whisper of gentle breathing).

15-MINUTE RELAXATION FOR AN ATTACK OF PANIC

Take yourself to a quiet, secluded room. Do a few minutes of slow stretch exercises to release some of the tension from your muscles. Then lie or sit in a well-supported position. Check that you are holding all your limbs in a loose position (for example, no crossed arms or legs or hunched shoulders!).

Close your eyes and visualize your breath passing into your body and through your lungs. Create a picture in your mind's eye of your heart throbbing as it pumps the oxygenated blood into your veins. Watch this pumping action gradually becoming slower and slower as you breathe more deeply and more evenly. Notice how your pulse has quietened.

Now tighten and very slowly release each of the following sets of muscles one by one:

toes ➔ calves ➔ thighs ➔ buttocks ➔ stomach ➔ chest ➔ shoulders ➔ fingers ➔ lower arms ➔ upper arms ➔ neck ➔ jaw ➔ eyes and forehead

Notice the sense of lightness in your body. Focus your attention back on your breathing for a few moments.

Now imagine you are on your own lying on a lilo in a quiet, sheltered pool in some beautiful garden location. The sun is warm but not burning and you are allowing yourself to gently float around in the water. The only sounds you can hear are the rustle of the nearby trees and some faint birdsong.

As you lie there in the pool, use your imagination to see yourself calming and successfully doing whatever it is you are wanting to do. Continue watching yourself for a few more minutes and feel in your body the sense of contentment and pleasure your achievement brings.

Slowly deepen your breathing and bring your attention back to the real world of the room where you have chosen to do this relaxation. Open your eyes and stay still for a few minutes before getting up.

- **Ensure that you timetable into your life a longer period (at least 30 to 60 minutes) of deeper relaxation once a week.** This could be merely an extended bath using a calming essence such as lavender. Alternatively, join a class of yoga, meditation or stretching, or engage in some de-stressing activity such as easy-going swimming, aimless walking or pottering in the garden. Once again, you will train your brain to associate this activity with being relaxed and then you can ensure you have a dose of it the day before you start doing whatever it is that you are dreading.

- **The evening before you need to get going on the dreaded activity, go to bed 10 minutes earlier that night.** Spend this time lying in a relaxed state with your eyes closed watching a 'mental movie' of you in confident action and not displaying any apparent fear.

- **List down the scenarios you dread.** (Did any of the common worries listed on pages 72–73 set you thinking?) Make a short contingency plan for each. Note what you could do to recover yourself or the situation should 'the worst' happen.

For example:

– **If I don't like it after all** – I will stop. Then I will analyze why with __ (a good friend or colleague) and use that wisdom to find something I will enjoy.

– **If I find I dry up in panic during a presentation** – I will take two deep breaths. Then I will visualize my relaxation scene (as discussed in the one-minute relaxation exercise on page 76); take a drink of water and make an assertive apology such as, *'Sorry, my mind went blank for a minute,'* and start again. (Every excellent presenter I know has done this more than once in their life!)

– **If I get too ill to continue** – I will delegate tasks to __. Then I will live off the more than adequate sickness insurance I have arranged until I am well. If I do not recover, I will contact a self-help group or association for people with that disability and draw on their inspiration, wisdom and support.

STEP 10

Use drama to stimulate passion for your dreams

Drama is a great means of stimulating passion. And don't you agree that you need much more of this powerful motivating force? I know that when it is stirring in me I am hardly likely to be sitting around reading a book on how to get going. (And no, I am not just referring to the pro-creational variety of passion!)

I know that being trained as a drama therapist I am perhaps a little biased on this subject. But I do believe that **drama is one of the most efficient and quickest ways to spice up your goals and transform them into dreams with drawing power.**

Most adults today have forgotten how useful creating a drama can be when it comes to drumming up more motivation. In modern westernized society it is mainly viewed as a recreational activity. It is used to bring us entertainment through, for example, theatrical productions, films and TV soaps. Some of you may also have experienced role-plays on training courses, but these rarely produce the kind of 'drama' which will stimulate the kind of feeling I am suggesting would help get you going. In my experience, there is usually more embarrassment than passion around! (Although, nevertheless, they are very useful for increasing intellectual awareness for rehearsing different styles of behaviour.)

If, however, you search back into your childhood memories, you will probably find plenty of examples of when you used the motivational power of drama – quite naturally and without, of course, realizing what you were doing!

- Can you recall how fired up with enthusiasm you felt when you were *playing* at being the driver of fire engines, ballerina, pop star, footballer, teacher or magician that you then wanted to become?
- Can you recall some of the vivid daydreams that you kept alive and running in your mind – and how you would silently return to these to keep

you going when adults forced you into boring
activities!
– Can you recall having an imaginary friend who
was real enough to you to get you to do or say
things which you would not have otherwise
dared do or say?
– Can you recall using dramatic voices, imperson-
ation and heavily 'embroidered facts' to motivate
your parents and friends to give you what you
wanted?

This step is essentially about re-harnessing
this very natural power of drama to rouse more
emotional commitment in you. You can use it to
transform your 'objectives' (such a sensible but
sterile word!) into vivid inspirational images. But
you can also use it to turn your nightmares into
garish visions that will serve as the wake-up calls
you need never have.

But I am aware that the reason some of you can't
get going is that you are still one step back from
setting yourself some specific goals. I would suggest
that you could still do some of these exercises
because dramatizing even vague ideas can be such
an enlightening way of exploring the potential

options to rouse the passion you need to follow
them through.

**Dramatizing your dreams will draw you
towards them.**

There are only two stimulants to one's best efforts: the fear of punishment and the hope of reward.

JOHN M. WILSON

Action time!

In the following exercise you will be using the energizing power of anger in a constructive way to fire you up. It can be done on your own (in privacy) or with an understanding friend (preferably one who also would like to try it themselves). Don't do it, however, if you think that you have such an inflammatory store of anger that you might harm someone or something. Instead, I suggest that you find an anger management course or a counsellor to help.

- **Take an empty chair and imagine yourself sitting in it.** While 'stomping' around the chair, act-out a temper tantrum at yourself. But be careful not to launch into an over-generalized personality attack. Instead, vent your feelings by expressing your frustration and anger using 'I' statements and listing examples of missed opportunities. (For example, *'I get so angry when you don't even explore the alternatives when one path gets blocked. John said "no" to your idea last week, but how do you know that that there weren't three others who would have said yes? – you didn't even ask'/'I couldn't believe you didn't take up that invitation to go out with Sarah even though you were tired.*

How do you know that it would just be the same old crowd in the pub again? For all you know Mr Right might have just dropped in and missed you yet again!' Describe in 'alarming' catastrophic detail the regrets, losses and difficulties that could lie ahead if you don't get going. (For example, *'Do you realize that ___will get that promotion instead of you and then ...'/'You are going to get so fat that ...'/'When your grandchildren ask what did you do when ... what will you say?'*)

Don't be afraid to use colourful exaggerations as long as your tirade doesn't become ridiculously unbelievable. It may help to warm yourself up for this exercise by making some notes for 'ammunition' beforehand. You could also try getting your adrenalin going by kicking a cushion around the chair. (But no punch bags – that might push your temper too near rage.)

• **When you have exhausted the subject (or yourself) do some deep breathing exercises and slow stretches to calm yourself down.** Make yourself a drink (not an alcoholic one!) and sit down and use your energy to set yourself a few *achievable* goals for the next week. If you still need to release more pent-up tension, expend it doing a much needed chore. (Not hard to spot the convent girl in me who was brought up on fire, brimstone and penance!)

- **In your mind's eye, set up an imaginary scene in ten years time which would symbolize your nightmare come true – i.e. the kind of situation you might be in if you don't get going now.** (For example, a scene of you doing what you are doing in your current work only looking a good deal more unhappy and prematurely aged / an image of you leading a single lonely life or living as a 'couch potato' watching the 'Dolce Vita' social life of others on your TV.) If you need inspiration for such a scene, just look around you – unfortunately it isn't hard to find living examples of disillusioned people who sold out on their dreams. Give this scene a snappy or silly name (like a title or chapter heading of a book such as 'Desperate Dan' or 'Lonesome Liz'). When your excuses show signs of getting the better of your good intentions, visualize the scene and say to yourself 'Beware ...!'. Share the image and name with a friend who can bring the nightmare into your consciousness for you as well.

- **Imagine yourself sometime in the future having successfully got going and now reaping the benefits from doing so.** Bring this best case scenario dramatically to life in one or more of the following ways:

  – **write a not-to-be-mailed letter to a friend or relative describing your dream life using the *present* tense.** Read this aloud several times in the next week, each time putting stronger inflection in your voice (as though you were perhaps reading a story to a young child you wanted to distract!)
  – **draw or paint a highly colourful picture or make a large collage of images from magazines to depict at least one scenario of your dream** (and no, you don't have to be *any* kind of artist to do this). Put the picture up where you will see it regularly and embellish or change it whenever you like. (Life-dreams should never be static – they should develop along with us and the circumstances that come our way.)
  – **act out your best case scenario with a few friends.** If you do this without the session descending into hamming-it-up hysteria, this

is the most powerfully effective way to dramatize your dream. I have used it successfully many hundreds of times to help others and myself. (No friends who'll comply? Then book yourself into a dramatherapy or psychodrama weekend workshop. A local search on the internet should produce a few possibilities.)

- **Keep your dream (not the nightmare – that's history!) alive by bringing it vividly into your imagination whenever you have an idle moment** (such as those times you are hanging around in stations and airports or standing in a queue in the bank). Also, talk about it regularly as though it is actually going to take place (for example, '*When* I …' not '*If* I …).

STEP 11

Come back down to earth with an achievable agenda

Back to your real world – of today, at least! Unfortunately, action plans are just as important to get yourself going as fantasy. (But please note, I didn't say *more* important – it is vital to still maintain daily contact with your dream.) They will always be an apparently less alluring task than daydreaming, but when you know the secrets they can be immensely satisfying and inspirational to do. And, of course, they are the essential 'engine' that drives us towards our vision. What you need to do now is to build your own 'Rolls Royce' version that will be a joy to drive. Think of this step as your deluxe DIY manual!

The three star secrets you need to keep in mind when building your achievable agenda are these:

1 **regard the task as a highly individualized art.**
The agenda that works for one person may be
completely wrong for another, even when they
have the exact same objective and are in identi-
cal circumstances. We each have our own best
method of working and a unique pace that main-
tains the right momentum for us. (If only more
parents and teachers acted as if they knew this!)
So it is important to keep focussed on what you
know is right for *you* and refrain from looking
over your shoulder at others' plans and progress.

2 **ensure that you build in effective progress
checks.** This will require a method of objective
measurement (as opposed to: *'I feel as though I'm
getting there'*). And for the artist to be humble
enough to include a way of obtaining candid
feedback. (Once we get going our enthusiasm
can be a bit blinding!)

3 **allow plenty of time for pleasurable rewards
throughout the course of the plan.** It is more
important to have rewards lined up for the small,
apparently insignificant achievements at the
start than it is to have a giant prize at the end.
(But of course, the ideal is to have both!)

Of course, you may not always be in circumstances that will allow you to build this Rolls Royce type of agenda. You could have an outline already set in stone by someone else (for example, a publisher with a deadline and team of people needing prompt delivery!). But aim for it whenever you can and make sure that you assert your right to negotiate – especially when circumstances change and you may need to shift the goalposts.

Inspiring action plans make the real world a very appealing place to live in.

Keep your eyes on the stars and your feet on the ground.

THEODORE ROOSEVELT

Action time!

- **Set a challenging and dated goal for yourself.**
  Your final outcome should be a result that fires
  your enthusiasm the moment you think about it.
  (Leave the very boring tasks well alone until you
  are stoked up with motivation.)

- **To check that your final outcome and time-
  frame are realistic and achievable, discuss
  them with friends or colleagues who can assess
  the feasibility of what it is you want to do.**
  These don't necessarily have to be people who
  know you well, they may be experts in the field of
  action you will be operating in (for example, a
  senior colleague at work, a sporting coach, an
  established author). This is important to do
  because setting unrealistic goals is another of
  those very common habits of unmotivated people.
  But before changing your goals or adding in
  other steps, check that their advice is objective
  and is not too shaped by their own individual
  experience. Asking a number of other people
  could help you in this respect, as could request-
  ing backup data such as any research findings or
  the results of similar projects, if available.

- **Note how you will be able to measure your progress.** Contact anyone who you may need to help you to do this (for example, someone who can help you devise an easy-to-read graphic chart to monitor the trend of your steps forward, or people who will give you honest feedback from their observations).

- **Set at least three mini-goals for yourself en route to your final outcome.** If possible make one to be achieved within the next week, even if it is a very simple one. For example:

  - **by the end of the week:** I will have made a phone call/bought a piece of equipment/ replaced the 'sinful' food in my fridge with healthy alternatives
  - **by the end of the month:** I will have had three relevant meetings/completed a business plan/lost one kilo
  - **in three months time:** I will have ten satisfied customers/learned how to use the tools/lost five kilos

- **List some rewards you could give yourself for each small step along the way towards your final goal.**

- **Write or type out your agenda in a way that gives you inspiration.** This could be setting it out in a very business-like manner or it making it look colourful and arty. Pin it up (together with your progress chart if you have made one) somewhere where it will be seen regularly.

Stage Four

making it easy to keep yourself going

So you are ready for action now, but there is probably still a foreboding voice in the back of your mind warning you that you are unlikely to keep going. Your work in this stage will hopefully quieten it once and for all! It will help you to take care that your environment remains as stimulating and supportive as it possibly can be and also prepare you to deal constructively with the inevitable distractions and dips in progress most of us meet. As a wannabe go-getter, you need to confront head-on these two hard truths. Firstly, that imperfection is part of the human-being package, and, secondly, unexpected challenges are a fact of life on earth. Your work in this stage should make these both easier to digest.

STEP 12

Create the most fruitful environment for action you can

Once upon a time I believed the myth that 'real' writers were artists who work enthusiastically and productively year after year in the grottiest and noisiest of freezing garrets. Now I know the reality. We are just like most other mortal workers! However inspired we are to produce our 'goods', and however big the 'carrots' are that are dangling in front of us, unless we have certain environmental conditions in which to do our job, it can be excruciatingly hard to *keep at* the task once the initial excitement of a new project has worn off. The only difference I see between us freelancing 'artisans' and the vast majority of other workers is that we usually have the privilege of being in charge of our working environment. So we can endlessly experiment until we find the one that works best for us.

I have just recently returned from a week on my own in our house in Spain where I have been very successfully writing.

You're going green because it sounds idyllic?

Well it is and it isn't. It is an ideal place to work because there I am spiritually and physically uplifted by the beauty and atmosphere of Andalucia. But on the minus side, it is very hard to isolate myself for a full week and deprive myself of my family and many of the other social pleasures that enrich my life in England. So working on my own in our house in Spain is not the perfect environment, but I go there because it gives me the best chance of producing quality work at the fastest rate.

How hard have you tried to give yourself the kind of environment which is highly conducive to action – at least most of the time?

My guess is that your honest answer is, 'Not hard enough'. I say this because I have often found that people who can't get going have been hampered by holding similar myths to mine in their heads. They too have only had eyes for the rare examples of the inspired saints in their field who are able to keep in action *wherever* and *whatever* the circumstances. (For example, the great inventor who produced the miracle in a cramped, cold shed, or the nurse who runs an efficient, happy ward in spite of overcrowding and air conditioning that eats up oxygen.) Perhaps, like them, you do not therefore grant yourself the 'luxury' of creating or campaigning for better work surroundings. But, in contrast, you may expend a great deal of energy trying to obtain rewards such as extra money and time off as compensation for grinding away in demotivating surroundings.

I recently heard a report on the radio about a piece of research that has proved that cows are more productive in a relaxing environment. 'Common sense' might be your understandable reaction to that piece of non-event news. But just how much of this kind of wisdom do you apply to your own working conditions? This step will help you judge that. You may not need or want the kind of environment that seems to suit the cows – and me! But if you want to maintain your motivation, you should at least make every attempt possible to ensure that your surroundings are well enough in tune with you and your task. Even though you may not be in charge of

your surroundings to the same extent as us free-
lancers, there are small changes that you can make
to your existing environment that will make a big difference to your motivation.

**Keep checking that your environment
is working in harmony with you and
your motivation.**

**To change yourself you first
have to change your surroundings.
A stimulating person lives and works
in a stimulating environment,
whilst a boring person lives
and works in a boring environment.**

DAVID FREEMANTLE

Action time!

- **Over the next week observe yourself in action within the environment in which you are operating.** (This could of course be a work one, or it could be home or a social setting.) Notice any frustrations or distractions or depressing features of your surroundings. For example:

  - traffic noise
  - uncomfortable chairs
  - bland colours
  - cluttered desk
  - coffee machine that makes foul-tasting coffee
  - overheated atmosphere (that is full of current cold viruses)
  - no views of outside world
  - litter

- **Make a list of what you need to do to improve your environment.** (For example, bring in some colour either with flowers or pictures/put aside a morning for a clearout/buy a book on Feng Shui/ask for the heating system to be serviced and turned down/start petition for upgrading of office, and so on.)

- **Take yourself away for a while to an inspiring environment.** This could be just an afternoon in a quiet library where you are surrounded by people who are studiously getting on with their tasks. Or it could be for a longer period to a place which you find uplifting because it is either beautiful, buzzing with action or one where you will be physically nurtured.

STEP 13

Get one-step ahead of your temptations

Unfortunately, all the hard work you have done to get going won't impress the devil. In fact, he might even see you in your inspirational environment as a juicer challenge. (Apologies for the gender bias in this step. Put it down to pure female prejudice!) As far as the satanic world is concerned, the 'holier' we are, the more interesting material we are. So expect the devil's alluring baits to burn brighter than ever before.

Sounds depressing? Then he is winning already! Don't let him. Get ready and prepared instead. Accept that you will be tempted to stray, off course.

You don't believe in devils?

Well, here is a more earthly explanation for the ratio-
nale behind the need for this step. Imagine, at last,
yourself in full action mode. You are excited; the end
of the tunnel is no longer invisible. Your self-esteem
is brimming over and you are elated by all the pleasurable inducement you have awarded yourself in
your effort to get going. In short, you are on a high!
The endorphins running through your system are
making you perceive the world as a good deal more
attractive than it did when you were feeling apathetic and frustrated with yourself. Maybe you have
even become so grandiose that you now believe you
can have your cake and eat it soaked in jam and
cream as well! In short, you have become overconfi-
dent in your motivation and think that you will easily
return to your task just as inspired as you were when
you left it.

At the same time you will be appearing more attractive to attractive others and feeling more attracted
towards them! Go-getters act like magnets for each
other. (Can't you just feel the strength of the energy
field that encircles them?) Instead of now feeling
intimidated by the people you have been admiring,
you will feel more on equal terms and will find them
and their projects and successes have a fascination

and an exciting pull. You will find yourself drawn more and more to wanting to spend time with them – if only to exchange ideas!

So I hope you can see that devil or no devil, once you get going you might find yourself sneaking off for the odd hour or two to indulge yourself just a little too often!

Don't completely deny yourself temptations – just get wised up enough to play with them on your terms.

The world is all the richer for having the devil in it, so long as we keep our foot on its neck.

WILLIAM JAMES

Action time!

- **List some of the temptations the devil may have stored up for you.** Beside each, note down what you may be able to do to help you resist them. For example:

  - *posters on the underground and train stations advertising films I want to see:* I could bury my head in a book I need to read or close my eyes and visualize my dream
  - *emails from friends sent to me during my working day:* I could choose not to read them but flag them and only reply during my last coffee break at the end of the day
  - *the soaps on TV which tempt me to waste evening after evening watching TV:* I could record them and then watch them as a reward for doing what I need to do
  - *must-have fashion clothes and shoes that will eat into my savings:* I could avoid going into town on Saturdays and ban magazines for six months

- **Note down the names of people who the devil may use as his aides.** (Perhaps imbuing them with extra enticing power!) Being 'on alert' will help you to resist any temptations these people may throw your way. For example:

– Gill: she could ring me up and invite me to join her on holiday. I know she's thinking of going to China and I've always wanted to go there
– Steve: he could ring me up to ask for help on his project. He is doing such leading-edge work now that I would find that hard to resist
– Mum: she could continue to cook me all those irresistible desserts

STEP 14

Prepare for unforeseeable pauses in progress

After all the work you have done in this strategy, I wish that I could give you a guarantee. It would give me so much pleasure to have the power to promise that the only time you will now stop going is when you choose to do so. But alas, I was not born to be divine and I guess neither were you. This means that our crystal balls will always have some cloudy, uncertain areas.

So, although I am confident that by taking the action I have suggested you have substantially increased your chances of keeping going, there could well be some unforeseen setbacks ahead that perhaps no mortal could hope to predict. For example:

- **your economic circumstances could change through no fault of your own.** (For example, through a new tax law; cutbacks at your place of work, or a sharp increase in the price of materials you need)
- **someone else could step in and sabotage your plans either consciously or unconsciously.** (For example, by preventing you from getting a resource you need because they are jealous; letting you down because they lose their motivation, or emotionally drawing you towards their needs which they believe have priority)
- **your level of physical energy could drop substantially even though you have been keeping fit.** (For example, through a contagious virus or an accident)
- **you could meet an unexpected trauma.** (For example, sickness of a child; a bereavement of a parent, or a natural disaster)

You would have to be very unusual to keep going without pausing in the face of any or some of these setbacks. You would also be very unwise to stop yourself from doing so. The first step in overcoming a setback has to be to take some time to calm your system. This is hard to do whilst still in motion!

So this step is not intended to deflate your ego or optimism, but simply to strengthen you more by bolstering you with the knowledge that you have the means and tools with which to bounce back into action.

Setbacks have the power to either strengthen or weaken your resolve – the choice is yours.

**Failure is only the opportunity to
begin again more intelligently.**

HENRY FORD

Action time!

- **Devise a means to set up an Emergency Fund especially for the purpose of getting you back on track.** This should include, if appropriate to your goal, some money to help you meet your everyday expenses. But, even more importantly, in relation to the subject of this book, there should be a sum set aside for lifting your spirits. The former resource most sensible people already have but not many think about the latter.

- **Prepare a store of ever-ready mood enhancers.** For example:

  - feel-good films on video
  - easy-reading books
  - positive-thinking cassettes/CDs
  - relaxation music
  - rousing music
  - fun exercise videos
  - comedy books
  - collection of motivational quotations
  - favourite affirmations written on attractive cards

- a 'celebration of me' book – containing photos and symbols which remind you of your strengths and successes
- a gratitude book – reminders of all the people and things in your life which you value and are likely to still be around
- mini-jobs that are easy to do and will happily divert your attention off your worries for a while
- nutritious and carbohydrate-rich foods to increase serotonin levels – that will keep for a long time, of course! (For example, pasta, rice and cereal)
- phone numbers and email addresses of friends who will give you support
- aromatherapy oils (bergamot, chamomile, lavender and orange are great for lifting the spirits)
- photo albums of beautiful places and buildings
- crossword or other puzzle books
- computer games, especially those which get the adrenalin going

Please note that I have not included alcohol in the above list. Why? Because for some people that may be just the very thing they do not need, but it is often the first thing they will turn to when they have a setback. (Don't I know that temptation!) Alcohol can be a great mood enhancer when we are feeling basically good and just need a mini-lift to relax us. But if we are down, it can (and usually will) make us even more depressed – even if that depression doesn't hit us until the hangover the following day. The same is true for many other drugs as well. That is why it is important to have other mood-enhancers already lined-up as alternatives.

STEP 15

Go selectively public with your plans

One of the tricks for sticking to resolutions is to inform the world of your good intentions. Fear of shame is, of course, usually the chief driving force operating here. But that shouldn't be the case with YOU. Your super self-esteem should be rendering you invulnerable to wounds to your pride. (Only joking – no-one's self-esteem can be that perfect!)

Speaking seriously though, you can use this trick but use it thoughtfully. You must choose the people who you tell with care. You should try to avoid telling people who:

- **want to see you fail.** (For example, those who could benefit from you not getting going or those who would get some satisfaction from

seeing you stay stuck because they have told you
many times you will never make it)

- **don't really care whether you get going or
not,** even if they may 'pay lip service' to support-
ing you. (For example, people who are too busy
or stressed doing their own thing, people who
don't really like you that much – even though
they may never admit to it)

Instead, choose people who:

- **do care about you**
- **can give you support en route** (if only the
morale-boosting kind)
- **will be thrilled if you do get going and want
to celebrate with you**
- **will still be there encouraging you if you do
make some slip-backs**

Perhaps this all sounds very obvious (and indeed it
should be after reading so far in this book!). But
because I have witnessed so many people making
mistakes in this area, I thought it would be useful for
you to check exactly how you are going to broadcast
your news.

You may want to bear in mind that the most common mistakes when looking for people to cheer us on are made close to home! Often our nearest and dearest are the ones who hold us back. Their doing so may not indicate a lack of love for us. It is often that they think that they know us too well! They have perhaps seen us stuck for so long that they find it hard to believe that we will ever get going. Or it could be simply that they are too stuck themselves. Change always brings fear and if our loved ones change it is even scarier – even though we may have been nagging them to change for the past 100 years! So you may have to get going in spite of their fear as well as your own. If this is the case, think about looking elsewhere (at least in the meantime) for your support.

Public announcements of your goals can help your commitment, but given to the wrong ears they will undoubtedly invite envy and scorn.

Keep your goals away from the trolls. People don't like to see others pursuing their dreams – it reminds them how far from living their dreams they are ... This, of course, does not apply to close friends and supporters who have always believed in you and offer only encouragement.

JOHN ROGER AND PETER MᶜWILLIAMS

Action time!

- **Reread the list on page 122 and then choose the people with whom it would be useful to share your plans.** They might be amongst those you chose to give you more smiles in Step 6, but they do not necessarily have to be. You could, for example, choose quite a serious minded colleague who has an investment in you getting going and has the skills to support you. Remember also to be honest with yourself when choosing – crossing someone off your list doesn't mean that they, or you, aren't a nice person!

- **Do an outline plan for a celebration party and share it with someone.** It may be too early at this stage to set a date and firm up an invitation list, but you could make some tentative arrangements or at least do some investigations. (For example, find a suitable date in your diary, research possible venues and special 'attractions'.) The friend you have chosen to share your ideas with can then remind you every so often what treat lies ahead! When my husband was recently made redundant we planned the celebration party we are about to have well before he had another job. Within a month of the 'bad news' we had selected the Flamenco artists we wanted to invite to give our party its buzz. We even thought through how we would manage the food with more limited means in case he had a major salary downshift (and he did – by choice!). I am not sure how influential the planning of this party was on my husband's motivation to get going again, but I do know it did it no harm and, without question, it provided both us and our friends with some welcome light relief amongst all the other more serious-minded planning and action.

A final word

I hope by now that you are feeling the buzz of excitement that being on the brink of committed action should bring. Of course you may still be a little nervous as well, that's natural. Just remember that you have cushioned yourself with inspiring support and have planned the route out of your worst-case scenario. You also know how to calm your pulse in the event of an attack of jitters and how to feed your self-esteem with sensual pleasure and mini-adventures should an attack of self-doubt begin to creep in.

Once you have got going and begun to feel more confidence in your ability to maintain your momentum, some of you may be interested in exploring even more ways of strengthening your self-motivational muscles. The following Further help section will give you some ideas of how you can do this.

I hope you have enjoyed this Shortcut strategy and, even more importantly, will enjoy that celebration party you have planned for yourself!

Further help

Recommended reading

Richard Carlson, *Don't Sweat the Small Stuff – and It's All Small Stuff* (Hodder and Mobius, 1998)

John Cook, *The Book of Positive Quotations* (Fairview Press, 1993)

David Freemantle, *The Stimulus Factor: The New Dimension in Motivation* (Prentice Hall, 2001)

John Gray, *How to Get What You Want and Want What You Have* (Vermilion 1999)

Robert Holden, *Shift Happens: Powerful Ways to Transform Your Life* (Hodder and Mobius, 2000)

Gael Lindenfield, *Assert Yourself* (Thorsons, 1986)

___, *Super Confidence* (Thorsons, 1989)

___, *The Positive Woman* (Thorsons, 1992)

___, *Managing Anger* (Thorsons, 1993)

___, *Self Esteem* (Thorsons, 1995)

___, *Self Motivation* (Thorsons, 1996)

___, *Emotional Confidence* (Thorsons, 1997)

___, *Success from Setbacks* (Thorsons, 1999)

___, *Confident Children* (Thorsons, 2000)

___, with Malcolm Vandenburg, *Positive Under Pressure* (Thorsons, 2000)

___, *Confident Teens* (Thorsons, 2001)

___, *Shortcuts to: Bouncing Back from Heartbreak* (Thorsons, 2002)

___, *Shortcuts to: Getting a Life* (Thorsons, 2002)

___, *Shortcuts to: Keeping Your Cool* (Thorsons, 2002)

___, *Shortcuts to: Making Hard Choices Easy* (Thorsons, 2002)

David McNally, *Even Eagles Need a Push* (Doubleday, 1994)

Cheryl Richardson, *Take Time for Your Life* (Bantam, 2001)

Anthony Robbins, *Awaken the Giant Within* (Simon and Schuster, 1992)

John Roger and Peter McWilliams, *Do it! A Guide to Living Your Dreams* (Thorsons, 1991)

Dorothy Rowe, *The Successful Self: Freeing Our Hidden Inner Strengths* (HarperCollins, 1989)

Dr P. D. Sharma, *Immortal Quotations and Proverbs*
    (Naveet Publications, 1999)
Paul Wilson, *Instant Calm* (Penguin, 1995)

Cassettes

Gael Lindenfield has made a number of personal-development cassettes. Each is designed as a self-help programme of exercises to be used on a regular basis. The list of titles includes:

- *Self Motivation* (Thorsons, 1997)
- *Self Esteem* (Thorsons, 1998)
- *Success from Setbacks* (Thorsons, 1999)
- *Managing Emotions at Work* (Thorsons, 1999)
- *Emotional Confidence* (Thorsons, 2000)

These cassettes are available at all good bookshops, or direct from Thorsons (telephone 0870 900 2050 or 0141 306 3349).

About the author

You can contact Gael Lindenfield through her
publishers at the following address:

Gael Lindenfield c/o Thorsons
HarperCollins*Publishers*
77–85 Fulham Palace Road
Hammersmith
London W6 8JB
United Kingdom

Or you can contact her directly by email:
lindenfield.office@btinternet.com

For further information about Gael Lindenfield and
her current programme, go to her website:
www.gael-lindenfield.com